Baby's Photograph

There is nothing quite like experiencing God's miracle of creation as you welcome your newborn into the world. The tiny hands, curled up toes, and velvety skin are a physical reminder of how fragile and wonderfully precious life really is.

Your baby's first year is an important time when you and your child begin to build a lifelong relationship based on mutual trust, love, understanding, and biblical principles. Each moment of this first year is a special event – from your baby's eager attempts at simple words to the day your child stands on wobbly little legs. Yet, with each day's busyness, the specifics of "when and where" – the unforgettable milestones – can be lost as other achievements quickly begin to mount up.

The Miracle of Life: Baby's First Year was created to capture these priceless moments in a beautifully designed record book. With delightful sections like Baby's Arrival, Bathtime and Water Play, First Christmas, and Plans and Prayers for the Future, you'll have a concise but thorough history of what is so often the most important year for a child. And years from now, or perhaps as an annual tradition together on your child's birthday, you'll be able to go back and read through this wonderful collection of memories, reliving each warm experience over and over again. God indeed does give us good things (Psalm 107:8-9) – and he wants us to joyfully celebrate them!

The Miracle OF LIFE

Baby's First Year

CONTENTS

JUBILEE PUBLISHING, INC.

Date and day of birth

Place of birth

B EFORE I FORMED YOU IN THE
WOMB, I KNEW YOU.
Jeremiah 1:5 NIV

Time of birth

Weight at birth

Length at birth

Color of eyes

Color of hair

Circumference of head

Name of Doctor

Description of the birth

Baby's appearance

....

Birth cards received

Every child born into the world
is a new thought of God,
an ever-fresh and radiant possibility.

Kate Douglas Wiggin

BABY'S FIRST PHOTOGRAPH

BIRTH ANNOUNCEMENT

FIRST DAYS

First visitors

Their comments

Feeding schedule

Baby's feeding times

Duration of a feeding

Description of a feeding

Sleeping schedule

Sleeping times

Wakeful times

Favorite sleeping position

Mother's feelings

Father's feelings

HUSH MY DEAR, LIE STILL AND SLUMBER,
HOLY ANGELS GUARD THY BED.
HEAVENLY BLESSINGS WITHOUT NUMBER
GENTLY FALLING ON THY HEAD.

Isaac Watts, *A Cradle Hymn*

Flowers received

PHOTOGRAPH

Gifts received

From whom

DEDICATION

INVITATION

Description of ceremony

Special guests

Gifts received

Your baby's behavior

Your baby's outfit

Scripture read

I PRAYED FOR THIS CHILD, SO NOW
I GIVE HIM TO THE LORD.

1 Samuel 1:27-28 NIV

FAMILY TREE

Maternal

Great-Grandmother
....
....

Great-Grandfather
....
....

Great-Grandmother
....
....

Great-Grandfather
....
....

Paternal

Great-Grandmother
....
....

Great-Grandfather
....
....

Great-Grandmother
....
....

Great-Grandfather
....
....

Grandmother
....
....

Grandfather
....
....

Grandmother
....
....

Grandfather
....
....

Mother
....

Father
....

Sisters
....

Baby
....

Brothers
....

— 7 —

FIRST FOODS

Most babies are introduced to solid foods at between three and six months old, and will relish discovering new tastes and textures.

H_E GIVES FOOD TO THOSE WHO TRUST HIM; HE ALWAYS REMEMBERS HIS COVENANT.

Psalm 111:5 NLT

God is great and God is good,
And we thank him for our food;
By his hand we are all fed,
Give us, Lord, our daily bread. Amen.

Date your baby first:

Ate puréed food

Ate solid food

Ate with a spoon

Ate in a high chair

Drank from a cup

Thank-you for the world so sweet,
Thank-you for the food we eat,
Thank-you for the birds that sing,
Thank-you, Lord, for everything. Amen.

— 8 —

Favorite food

Description of a meal

Date of weaning

TEETHING

ADAM AND EVE HAD MANY ADVANTAGES, BUT THE PRINCIPAL ONE WAS THAT THEY ESCAPED TEETHING.

Mark Twain

A baby cuts 20 primary or milk teeth, which begin to be replaced with permanent teeth when the child is about six years old. The appearance of the first tooth is a milestone in a baby's life, although it can cause a great deal of discomfort. Some babies find chewing on a teething ring soothes the gums and helps lessen the pain.

Date of first tooth

Date of second tooth

Date of third tooth

Date of fourth tooth

Date of fifth tooth

Teething symptoms

Notes

Top teeth

Teething order

Bottom teeth

— NIGHT-TIME —

CHILDREN ARE A GIFT FROM THE LORD; THEY ARE A REWARD FROM HIM.

Psalm 127:3 NLT

Bedtime

Favorite sleeping position

Wakes at

Bedtime comforters

First sleeps through night

First sleeps in crib

Now I lay me down to sleep
In my Father's tender care.
I pray for quiet, soothing rest,
And sweetest dreams of
my Savior fair.

JESUS LOVES ME, THIS I KNOW
FOR THE BIBLE TELLS ME SO
LITTLE ONES TO HIM BELONG
THEY ARE WEAK, BUT HE IS STRONG.

Anna B. Warner

Description of cot

Description of nursery

Notes

Sleep sound in Jesus,
My baby, my dear.
Angels are watching;
They keep you so near.

Favorite lullabies

Favorite bed time toys

Golden slumbers kiss your eyes;
Smiles awake you when you rise;
Sleep, pretty baby, do not cry,
And I will sing you a lullaby.

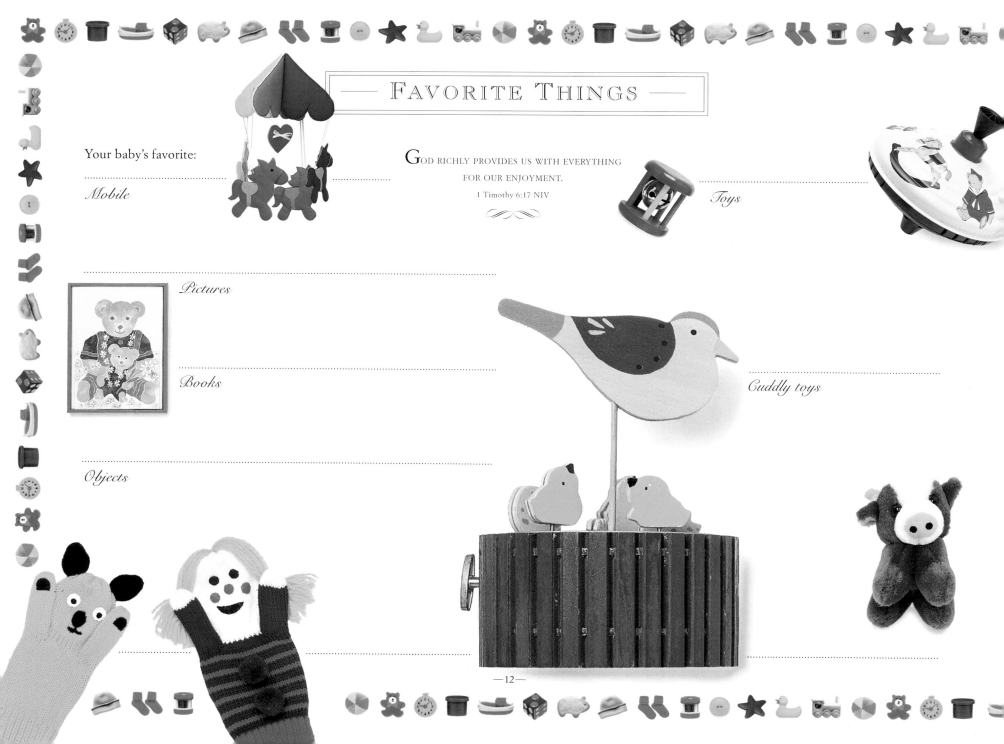

FAVORITE THINGS

Your baby's favorite:

Mobile

....

GOD RICHLY PROVIDES US WITH EVERYTHING
FOR OUR ENJOYMENT.

1 Timothy 6:17 NIV

Toys

....

Pictures

....

Books

Cuddly toys

....

Objects

....

—12—

Games

Activities

Sounds

Words

People

Animals

Stories

Songs and Nursery Rhymes

ALL THINGS BRIGHT AND BEAUTIFUL,
ALL CREATURES, GREAT AND SMALL,
ALL THINGS WISE AND WONDERFUL,
THE LORD GOD MADE THEM ALL.
Cecil Frances Alexander

— Bathtime and Water Play —

First enjoys bath

....

First time in a big bathtub

....

Response to being bathed

....

Response to hair being washed

....

Let the head grow wise,
but keep the heart always
young and playful.

David Livingstone

Favorite bath toys

....

Bathtime activities

....

*R*ow, row, row your boat
Gently down the stream
Merrily, merrily, merrily, merrily,
Life is but a dream.

*O*ne, two, three, four, five,
Once I caught a fish alive,
Six, seven, eight, nine, ten,
Then I let him go again.
Why did you let him go?
Because he bit my finger so.
Which finger did he bite?
This little finger on the right.

First water play in garden

First play in wading pool

First swim in swimming pool

Your baby's swimwear

PHOTOGRAPH

Favorite water games

FIRST OUTINGS

Details of first trips made by:

Car

Train

> THERE ARE TWO CLASSES OF TRAVEL –
> FIRST CLASS, AND WITH CHILDREN.
> Robert Benchley

Bus

Airplane

Boat

Outings to:

Grandparents

Relatives

Special friends

> EVERY MOMENT, YOU KNOW WHERE I AM.
> YOU BOTH PRECEDE AND FOLLOW ME, AND PLACE
> YOUR HAND OF BLESSING ON MY HEAD.
> Psalm 139:3, 5 NLT

Outings to:

Parks and playgrounds

Beaches or cities

The countryside

Church

GOD MADE LIFE A LITTLE LIGHT,
WITHIN THE WORLD TO GLOW;
A TINY FLAME THAT BURNETH BRIGHT,
WHEREVER I MAY GO.

M. Bentham-Edwards

Notes

PHOTOGRAPH

FIRST CHRISTMAS

F OR TO US A CHILD IS BORN,
TO US A SON IS GIVEN.

Isaiah 9:6 NIV

Christmas Day:

Where it was spent

Who it was spent with

Your present to your baby

Stocking gifts

Gifts received

From whom

Description of the holidays

A way in a manger,
no crib for a bed,
The little Lord Jesus
laid down His sweet head;
The stars in the sky
looked down where he lay,
The little Lord Jesus,
asleep on the hay.

Christmas Eve:

Where it was spent

Who it was spent with

Description of Christmas Eve

Favorite Christmas presents

Family Christmas activities

Favorite Christmas games

Description of the Christmas tree

PHOTOGRAPH

Christmas weather

Notes

FIRST VACATION

Date

Place

Who was there

Travel details

Accommodation

Favorite activities

Favorite outings

Baby's behavior

Baby's new friends

PHOTOGRAPH

Favorite memories of the vacation

Notes

IT IS A HAPPY TALENT TO KNOW HOW TO PLAY.
Ralph Waldo Emerson

FIRST BIRTHDAY

Date ....

How celebrated ....

Who was there ....

Description of cake ....

Your baby's outfit ....

Gifts received ....

YOU ARE PRECIOUS AND
HONORED IN MY SIGHT,
AND I LOVE YOU.
Isaiah 43:4 NIV

Your present ....

Your baby's behavior

*H*appy birthday to you
Happy birthday to you
Happy birthday dear baby
Happy birthday to you.

PHOTOGRAPH

Notes

─MILESTONES─

A CHILD MORE THAN ALL OTHER GIFTS
THAT GOD CAN OFFER TO MAN
BRINGS HOPE WITH IT, AND
FORWARD-LOOKING THOUGHTS.

William Wordsworth

First smiles

First discovers hands and feet

First grasps object

First holds head up

First sits up

First kiss

First haircut

First solid food

First tooth

First crawls

First stands

First steps

First waves goodbye

First words

First says Mama

First says Dada

WE FIND DELIGHT IN THE BEAUTY AND
HAPPINESS OF CHILDREN THAT MAKES THE
HEART TOO BIG FOR THE BODY.

Ralph Waldo Emerson

First recognizes:

Mother

Father

Grandparents

Special friends

Animals

First friends

PHOTOGRAPH

Notes

MEMENTOS

Identification tag from hospital

Footprints

Handprints

P ARENTS ARE GARDENERS – PLANTING THE SEEDS OF FAITH, TRUTH, AND LOVE THAT DEVELOP INTO THE
FAIREST FLOWERS OF CHARACTER, VIRTUE, AND HAPPINESS IN THE LIVES OF THEIR CHILDREN.

J. Harold Gwynne

Lock of hair

Special treasures

MEDICAL RECORD

THE LORD WILL GUIDE YOU CONTINUALLY, WATERING YOUR LIFE
WHEN YOU ARE DRY AND KEEPING YOU HEALTHY, TOO.

Isaiah 58:11 NLT

Immunization details

Vaccine	Age	Date
*Diphtheria	Tetanus	Pertussis*		
Polio		
Hemophilus b		
*Measles	Mumps	Rubella*		
Other		

Illnesses

Diagnosis	Age	Date

Visits to doctor

Reason   *Age*   *Date*

....

....

....

....

....

....

....

....

Allergies

....

Blood group

....

Eyesight test

....

Hearing test

....

AGE AND WEIGHT CHART

Weight   Age in months

lbs	kgs	0	1	2	3	4	5	6	7	8	9	10	11	12

———— Average for girls
———— Average for boys

Notes

SPECIAL MEMORIES

Of all the wonderful things to have happened during your baby's first year of life, some will stand out as particularly memorable and worth recording.

KIDS ARE GREAT. THEY ARE EXCITING.
AND THEY CAN CHANGE THIS WORLD FOR GOD.

Maxine Hancock, *Creative, Confident Children*

PLANS AND PRAYERS
FOR THE FUTURE

....

Dreams for your baby

....

Possible schools

....

Character traits & skills you've noticed

....

Prayers for your baby's future

For I know the plans I have for you," declares the
Lord, "plans to give you hope and a future."

Jeremiah 29:11 NIV

PHOTOGRAPH

FROM   TO

DAY
1

Date..........................

DAY
2

DAY
3

DAY
4

DAY
5

DAY
6

DAY
7

DAY
8

DAY
9

DAY
10

DAY
11

DAY
12

DAY
13

DAY
14

DAY
15

DAY
16

DAY
17

DAY
18

DAY
19

DAY
20

DAY
21

DAY
22

DAY
23

DAY
24

DAY
25

DAY
26

DAY
27

DAY
28

DAY
29

DAY
30

DAY
31

FROM .... TO. ....

Weight ....

Length ....

Sleeping pattern ....

....

Bedtime ....

Feeding pattern ....

....

Physical changes ....

....

Medical checkups ....

....

New sounds ....

....

Response to mother ....

....

Response to father ....

....

PHOTOGRAPH

Date of photograph ....

A typical day ....

....

FROM   TO

PHOTOGRAPH

Weight

Length

Sleeping pattern

Bedtime

Feeding pattern

Physical changes

Medical checkups

New sounds

Date of photograph

A typical day

Response to mother

Response to father

FROM   TO

....

DAY 1	DAY 2	DAY 3	DAY 4	DAY 5	DAY 6	DAY 7
Date............................						
DAY 8	DAY 9	DAY 10	DAY 11	DAY 12	DAY 13	DAY 14
DAY 15	DAY 16	DAY 17	DAY 18	DAY 19	DAY 20	
DAY 21	DAY 22	DAY 23	DAY 24	DAY 25	DAY 26	
DAY 27	DAY 28	DAY 29	DAY 30	DAY 31		

FROM .... TO ....

DAY 1	DAY 2	DAY 3	DAY 4	DAY 5	DAY 6	DAY 7
Date........................						
DAY 8	DAY 9	DAY 10	DAY 11	DAY 12	DAY 13	
DAY 14	DAY 15	DAY 16	DAY 17	DAY 18	DAY 19	DAY 20
DAY 21	DAY 22	DAY 23	DAY 24	DAY 25	DAY 26	
DAY 27	DAY 28	DAY 29	DAY 30	DAY 31		

FROM .... TO ....

Weight .... Length ....

Sleeping pattern ....

....

Wakes up ....

Bedtime ....

Feeding pattern ....

Medical checkups ....

Physical changes ....

....

New sounds ....

....

Response to mother ....

Response to father ....

A typical day ....

....

PHOTOGRAPH

Date of photograph

FROM   TO

Weight   Length

Sleeping pattern

Wakes up

Bedtime

Description of mealtime

Physical changes

New movements

New sounds

Medical checkups

Favorite activities

A typical day

PHOTOGRAPH

Date of photograph

FROM   TO
....

DAY 1 Date............................	DAY 2	DAY 3	DAY 4	DAY 5	DAY 6	DAY 7
DAY 8	DAY 9	DAY 10	DAY 11	DAY 12	DAY 13	DAY 14
	DAY 15	DAY 16		DAY 17	DAY 18	
DAY 19	DAY 20	DAY 21		DAY 22	DAY 23	DAY 24
DAY 25	DAY 26	DAY 27	DAY 28	DAY 29	DAY 30	DAY 31

FROM .... TO ....

DAY 1	DAY 2	DAY 3	DAY 4	DAY 5	DAY 6	DAY 7
Date	DAY 8	DAY 9	DAY 10	DAY 11	DAY 12	DAY 13
	DAY 14	DAY 15	DAY 16	DAY 17		DAY 18
DAY 19	DAY 20	DAY 21	DAY 22	DAY 23		DAY 24
DAY 25	DAY 26	DAY 27	DAY 28	DAY 29	DAY 30	DAY 31

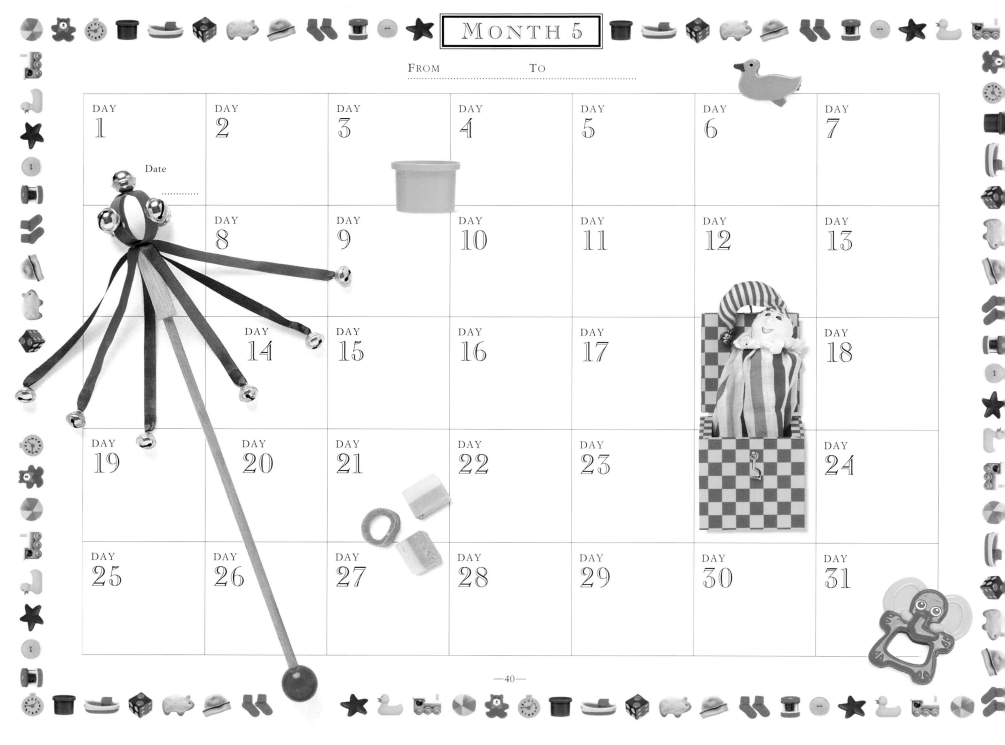

FROM .... TO ....

Weight ....

Length ....

Sleeping pattern ....

Wakes up ....

Bedtime ....

Description of mealtime ....

Favorite foods ....

Medical checkups ....

PHOTOGRAPH

Date of photograph ....

New movements ....

Favorite outing ....

Physical changes ....

A typical day ....

New sounds ....

Favorite activities ....

FROM

TO

Weight

Length

Sleeping pattern

Wakes up

Bedtime

Description of mealtime

Favorite foods

Medical checkups

PHOTOGRAPH

Date of photograph

Favorite outing

A typical day

New movements

Physical changes

New sounds

Favorite activities

FROM .... TO ....

DAY 1	DAY 2	DAY 3	DAY 4	DAY 5	DAY 6
Date.........................					
DAY 7	DAY 8	DAY 9	DAY 10	DAY 11	DAY 12	DAY 13
DAY 14	DAY 15	DAY 16	DAY 17	DAY 18	DAY 19	DAY 20
DAY 21	DAY 22		DAY 23	DAY 24	DAY 25	
DAY 26	DAY 27	DAY 28	DAY 29	DAY 30	DAY 31	

FROM .... TO ....

DAY
1

Date....................

DAY
2

DAY
3

DAY
4

DAY
5

DAY
6

DAY
7

DAY
8

DAY
9

DAY
10

DAY
11

DAY
12

DAY
13

DAY
14

DAY
15

DAY
16

DAY
17

DAY
18

DAY
19

DAY
20

DAY
21

DAY
22

DAY
23

DAY
24

DAY
25

DAY
26

DAY
27

DAY
28

DAY
29

DAY
30

DAY
31

FROM .... TO ....

Weight ....

Length ....

Sleeping pattern ....

....

Wakes up ....

Bedtime ....

Description of mealtime ....

....

Favorite foods ....

Medical checkups ....

New movements ....

Physical changes ....

New sounds ....

Favorite activities ....

PHOTOGRAPH

Date of photograph ....

Favorite outing ....

A typical day ....

....

—45—

FROM .... TO ....

PHOTOGRAPH

Weight

Length

Sleeping pattern

Wakes up

Bedtime

Description of mealtime

Favorite foods

Medical checkups

Date of photograph

Favorite outing

A typical day

New movements

Physical changes

New sounds

Favorite activities

FROM   TO

....

DAY 1	DAY 2	DAY 3	DAY 4	DAY 5	DAY 6	DAY 7
Date.............						
DAY 8	DAY 9	DAY 10	DAY 11	DAY 12	DAY 13	DAY 14
DAY 15		DAY 16	DAY 17	DAY 18	DAY 19	DAY 20
DAY 21	DAY 22	DAY 23	DAY 24	DAY 25	DAY 26
DAY 27	DAY 28	DAY 29	DAY 30	DAY 31		

FROM .... TO

DAY 1	DAY 2	DAY 3	DAY 4	DAY 5		DAY 6
Date..................						
DAY 7	DAY 8	DAY 9	DAY 10	DAY 11	DAY 12	DAY 13
DAY 14	DAY 15	DAY 16	DAY 17	DAY 18	DAY 19	DAY 20
DAY 21	DAY 22	DAY 23	DAY 24	DAY 25		
DAY 26	DAY 27	DAY 28	DAY 29	DAY 30	DAY 31	

MONTH 9

FROM .... TO ....

Weight .... Length ....

Sleeping pattern ....

....

Wakes up ....

Bedtime ....

Description of mealtime ....

....

Physical changes ....

....

New movements ....

....

New sounds ....

....

Medical checkups ....

Favorite activities ....

....

A typical day ....

....

PHOTOGRAPH

Date of photograph

FROM   TO

Weight   Length

Sleeping pattern

Wakes up

Bedtime

Description of mealtime

Physical changes

New movements

New sounds

Medical checkups

Favorite activities

A typical day

PHOTOGRAPH

Date of photograph

FROM .... TO ....

DAY 1	DAY 2	DAY 3	DAY 4	DAY 5	DAY 6	DAY 7
Date............................						
DAY 8	DAY 9	DAY 10	DAY 11	DAY 12	DAY 13	DAY 14
DAY 15		DAY 16	DAY 17	DAY 18	DAY 19	
DAY 20	DAY 21	DAY 22	DAY 23	DAY 24	DAY 25	
DAY 26	DAY 27	DAY 28	DAY 29	DAY 30	DAY 31	

FROM .... TO ....

DAY 1	DAY 2	DAY 3	DAY 4	DAY 5	DAY 6	DAY 7
Date..........................						
DAY 8	DAY 9	DAY 10	DAY 11		DAY 12	DAY 13
DAY 14	DAY 15	DAY 16	DAY 17	DAY 18	DAY 19	DAY 20
DAY 21	DAY 22	DAY 23	DAY 24	DAY 25	DAY 26	
	DAY 27	DAY 28	DAY 29	DAY 30	DAY 31	

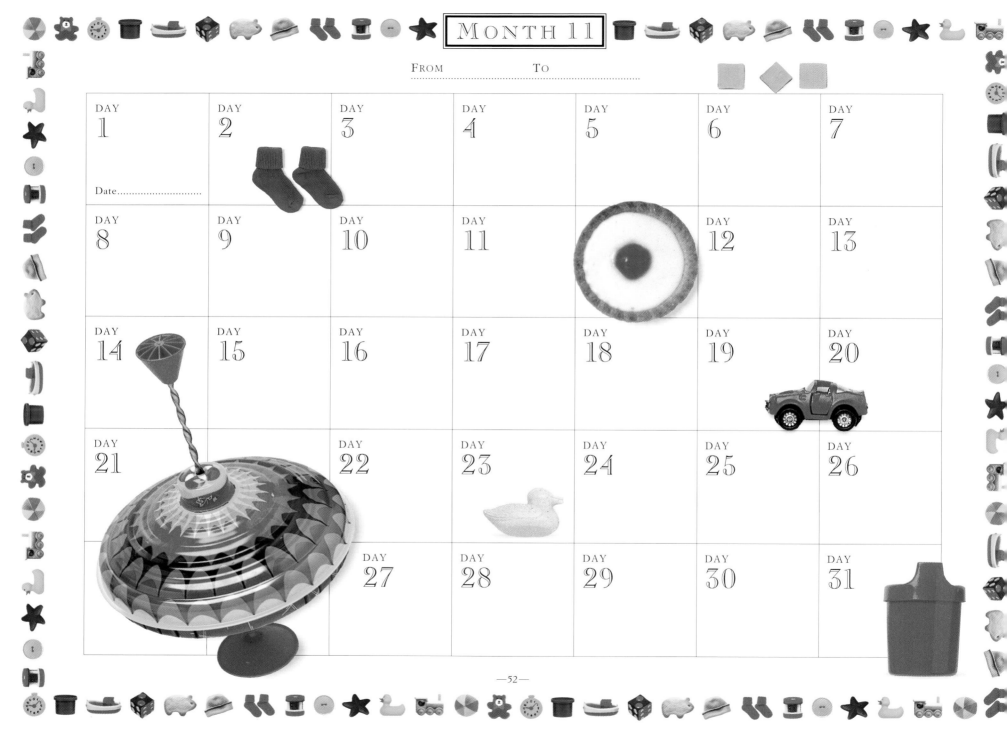

FROM .... TO ....

Weight ....

Length ....

Sleeping pattern ....
....

Wakes up ....

Bedtime ....

Description of mealtime ....
....
....

Favorite foods ....
....

Medical checkups ....

PHOTOGRAPH

Date of photograph ....

New movements ....

Physical changes ....

New sounds ....

Favorite activities ....

Favorite outing ....

A typical day ....

FROM

TO

PHOTOGRAPH

Weight

Length

Sleeping pattern

Wakes up

Bedtime

Description of mealtime

Favorite foods

Medical checkups

Date of photograph

Favorite outing

A typical day

New movements

Physical changes

New sounds

Favorite activities

FROM .... TO ....

DAY
1

Date.............................

DAY
2

DAY
3

DAY
4

DAY
5

DAY
6

DAY
7

DAY
8

DAY
9

DAY
10

DAY
11

DAY
12

DAY
13

DAY
14

DAY
15

DAY
16

DAY
17

DAY
18

DAY
19

DAY
20

DAY
21

DAY
22

DAY
23

DAY
24

DAY
25

DAY
26

DAY
27

DAY
28

DAY
29

DAY
30

DAY
31

A Dorling Kindersley book

Design Bernard Higton

First published in Great Britain in 1995 by
Dorling Kindersley Limited,
9 Henrietta Street, London WC2E 8PS

This edition published in the United States by
Jubilee Publishing, Inc.
Post Office Box 30
Lebanon, TN 37088

To order, contact:
Christian Network International, Inc. (CNI)
5584 Mountain View Road
Nashville, TN 37013-2311
Phone: (800) 933-7161
FAX: (615) 641-5566

ISBN 1-57727-105-X

Color reproduction by Colourscan, Singapore
Printed and bound by Tien Wah Press, Singapore

04 03 02 01 00 99 98
8 7 6 5 4 3 2 1